Who Was
Alexander Hamilton?

by Pam Pollack and Meg Belviso

illustrated by Dede Putra

Penguin Workshop
An Imprint of Penguin Random House

For Bill Blakeslee, tax wizard—PP

For Tom Belviso, founding father—MB

PENGUIN WORKSHOP
Penguin Young Readers Group
An Imprint of Penguin Random House LLC

Text copyright © 2017 by Pam Pollack and Meg Belviso. Illustrations copyright © 2017 by Penguin Random House LLC. All rights reserved. Published by Penguin Workshop, an imprint of Penguin Random House LLC, 345 Hudson Street, New York, New York 10014. PENGUIN and PENGUIN WORKSHOP are trademarks of Penguin Books Ltd. WHO HQ & Design is a registered trademark of Penguin Random House LLC. Printed in the USA.

Library of Congress Cataloging-in-Publication Data is available.

ISBN 9780399544279 (paperback)   10 9 8 7 6 5 4 3 2
ISBN 9780399544293 (library binding)   10 9 8 7 6 5 4 3 2

Contents

Who Was Alexander Hamilton?

On July 11, 1804, high above the Hudson River in Weehawken, New Jersey, two men met at dawn. They were Alexander Hamilton, a Revolutionary War hero and the first secretary of the treasury, and Aaron Burr, the vice president of the United States. They had come to fight a duel.

In the early 1800s, dueling was common. When two gentlemen got into a fight that they couldn't settle with words, they agreed to meet with pistols instead. In a secluded place, they faced each other. They planned to point and shoot at the same time. If they were lucky, both men would survive. The men stood on a high rock cliff facing the water. They were hidden by trees. This was a popular spot for duels.

A man who refused to fight a duel was seen as a coward. But dueling was illegal in New York City, where Alexander and Aaron lived. New Yorkers could be punished for dueling. That is why they had come to Weehawken—a spot right across the river from New York City. New Jersey was not as strict about dueling.

Alexander Hamilton and Aaron Burr had known each other for many years. Sometimes they worked together as lawyers or in the government. Often they disagreed. A few weeks earlier, Alexander had insulted Aaron at a dinner party. Aaron demanded an apology when he found out, but Alexander refused. Friends of the two men tried to make peace between them. But it was no use.

Alexander Hamilton and Aaron Burr raised their pistols and took their aim. Only one would survive.

CHAPTER 1
A Caribbean Childhood

On January 11, 1755, Alexander Hamilton was born on Nevis, a small island in the West Indies. It is now part of the country called the Federation of Saint Kitts and Nevis. It was a British colony, which meant it was governed by Great Britain and its king, George III.

Alexander's parents were James Hamilton and Rachel Faucette. James had grown up in Scotland, where his family lived in a castle. But as the youngest son, James didn't inherit it. He came to the West Indies hoping to make money, but he wasn't very good at it.

Rachel Faucette had been born in the West Indies, and her family was French. James and Rachel were not married. Rachel had married another man when she was young, but he was very mean. She ran away, leaving behind a son, and she never saw him again. Rachel and James lived together as husband and wife and had two children, James and Alexander.

The West Indies

When Christopher Columbus set out from Spain, he hoped to sail west and eventually find the islands known as "the East Indies." The place that Columbus was really looking for was east of Spain, in the Pacific Ocean—a country we now call Indonesia. When he came upon a group of islands in the Caribbean, he thought he had reached his

destination. So he called these islands "the Indies." When people realized Columbus's mistake, they referred to this area of the Atlantic Ocean as the West Indies.

Also known as the Caribbean Basin, the West Indies encompass the triangle from Florida south along the coast of Central America, eastward along the coast of South America, and northward to Bermuda.

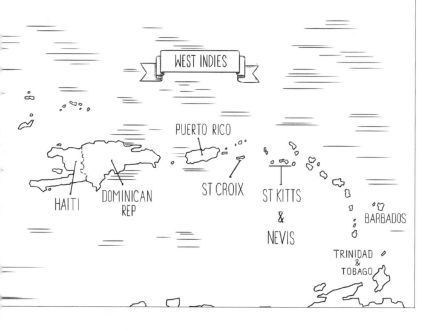

WEST INDIES

PUERTO RICO

HAITI

DOMINICAN REP

ST CROIX

ST KITTS & NEVIS

BARBADOS

TRINIDAD & TOBAGO

Many white people on the island made money by growing sugarcane. Most of the sugarcane was picked by slaves who had been brought to the islands from Africa. It was a terrible job, standing in the hot sun and harvesting the plants. So terrible that many slaves died within five years of being sent to the island. Perhaps it was seeing people suffer this way that turned Alexander against slavery for the rest of his life.

Alexander loved to read both in English and French, a language he learned from his mother. He probably wasn't allowed to go to a formal school because his parents weren't married, so he was tutored. But in his small town, Alexander and James didn't really think of themselves as different from other children. It wasn't unusual for boys to be taught at home.

The Triangle Trade

Sugarcane is a type of grass that grows over six feet tall. It grows best in tropical climates, but it did not exist in the West Indies until Christopher Columbus brought it there. Europeans saw this as a good place to raise the crop, using slaves as free labor.

Ships left European ports and sailed to Africa carrying valuable items like guns, cloth, and copper. Once in Africa, they would trade goods for human beings who would later be sold as slaves. Many died on the journey, but those who survived were brought to America to work on plantations and pick cotton, or sent to the Caribbean to harvest sugarcane.

NORTH AMERICA

THE CARIBBEAN

The cotton and the sugar—often in the form of molasses or rum—was shipped back to Europe. Because the ships returned to the same three areas over and over, this was called the Triangle Trade.

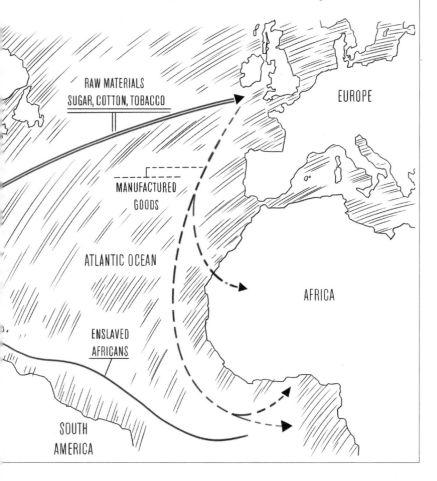

RAW MATERIALS
SUGAR, COTTON, TOBACCO

EUROPE

MANUFACTURED
GOODS

ATLANTIC OCEAN

AFRICA

ENSLAVED
AFRICANS

SOUTH
AMERICA

In 1765, James Hamilton moved the family to another island, called St. Croix (say: saint CROY), which today is part of the United States Virgin Islands. In St. Croix, Alexander and his brother, James, started to understand for the first time that they were different from other children because their parents weren't married. Some people on the island did not approve.

In 1766, when Alexander was eleven years old, his father abandoned the family. He didn't think he could support them anymore and went off to one of the other islands to try to earn more money. A year later Alexander and his mother got very sick. No one knows what the illness was, but for days they both lay in bed burning with fever. Alexander recovered but his mother died.

James and Alexander went to live with an adult cousin but he, too, died within just a few years. Now the boys were truly alone in the world.

Everything their mother had owned belonged
to her first husband. So the boys were left with
nothing. With their mother dead and their
father gone, they had no idea what their future
would hold.

CHAPTER 2
A Remarkable Boy

Alexander's brother, James, was apprenticed to a carpenter on St. Croix. That meant he would live with the carpenter and eventually learn to be one himself. He and Alexander never saw each other again. Alexander was taken in by

Thomas Stevens, a merchant who lived on the island. Thomas had five children of his own and one, Edward, was a year older than Alexander. Alexander and Edward, called Ned, became the best of friends.

Although he was only thirteen, Alexander was given a job as a clerk in a mercantile house, a business that traded and shipped goods all over the world. Alexander was determined to learn everything he could about the business. He was very good at math and had no trouble keeping track of all the money and products that came in and went out. He was so good at his job that when one of the owners went to New York for five months, he left Alexander in charge of the entire business. Alexander was only fourteen years old.

Although he was doing well at his job, Alexander didn't want to work there forever. He dreamed of leaving the West Indies and becoming famous, maybe joining an army and becoming a war hero. He longed to follow Ned Stevens to New York, where his friend was going to school to become a doctor, but Alexander didn't have the money to travel.

In 1770, St. Croix's first newspaper, the *Royal Danish American Gazette*, was published. Alexander was excited to write for it. In 1771, when he was sixteen, he published two love poems in the paper. More poems followed.

Another part-time writer at the paper was a minister named Hugh Knox. He and Alexander became friends.

On August 31, 1772, a terrible hurricane hit the island of St. Croix. Roaring winds knocked down trees, and a tidal wave over fifteen feet high pounded the shores.

The *Gazette* described it as "the most dreadful hurricane known in the memory of man." The hurricane was so big, it caused destruction on the neighboring islands of St. Kitts and Nevis as well.

A few days later, at a Sunday service, Hugh Knox preached a sermon about the hurricane. Alexander was inspired to write his own version of the story in a letter to his father. James Hamilton was probably living on an island just outside the range of the hurricane. Alexander wrote a dramatic letter describing all the horrors of the storm. Before sending the letter, he showed it to his friend Hugh.

The minister was impressed. Hugh thought it was so good that Alexander should publish it in the paper. The *Gazette* printed Alexander's letter on October 3, 1772, with an introduction by Hugh Knox explaining that its author was still just a teenager.

In part, the letter read: "The roaring of the sea and wind, fiery meteors flying about in the air, the prodigious glare of almost perpetual lightning, the crash of the fallen houses, and the ear-piercing shrieks of the distressed, were sufficient to strike astonishment into Angels."

Alexander's letter was an unexpected hit with the people of St. Croix. Everyone was impressed

by how well it was written. They thought he had really captured the force and destruction of the hurricane. Many wealthy people decided to take up a collection to send Alexander to America so that he could go to college. A boy who could write such a letter, they thought, should not stay on their little island. He should have a chance to make his mark on the world.

Alexander Hamilton was going to New York.

CHAPTER 3
King's College

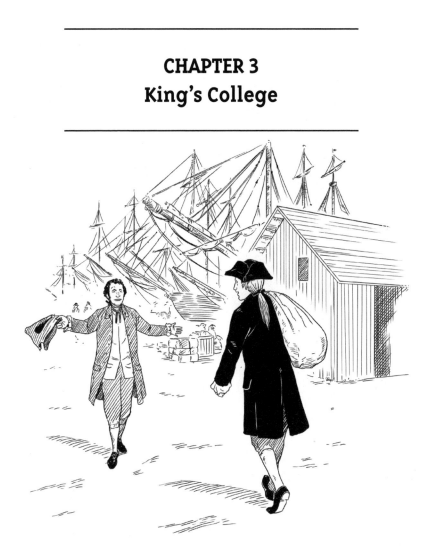

Alexander arrived in New York City in 1773. Ned Stevens was waiting for him there.

Alexander also quickly made friends with a young tailor named Hercules Mulligan. Hugh Knox had written to friends he knew in New York, so Alexander met even more people through him. He enrolled in the Elizabethtown Academy in New Jersey, where he studied Latin, Greek, and advanced math. After six months, he was ready to apply to college.

Now known as Princeton University, the College of New Jersey had been Alexander's first choice. Although he was only eighteen, he felt his education was way behind other young men his age. Alexander had heard of another young man, Aaron Burr, who graduated from the College of New Jersey at sixteen. So he asked the president of the college if he could complete his studies in only two years. He wanted to graduate as quickly as he could. The president refused, so Alexander enrolled in another school: King's College in New York City, which is now called Columbia University.

King's College

At King's College, everyone was talking about revolution. New York at that time was one of thirteen colonies owned by Great Britain. Like Alexander's home in Nevis, it was under the control of the British king, George III. Many colonists were angry that the king taxed the colonies for their money but did not give them a voice in the government.

KING GEORGE III

The president of King's College, Dr. Myles Cooper, was a Tory. The Tory party thought the American colonies should be loyal to Britain. But Alexander believed in American independence from Britain. Just outside the college grounds, on lower Broadway in Manhattan, was an area called the Fields. Anyone was welcome to make public speeches there. Alexander had listened to many speakers at the Fields. One day he decided to speak himself. He started out shyly. He'd never spoken in public before. But soon he was making a powerful argument against the rule of Great Britain in the colonies.

When he finished, the crowd was shocked at first. Alexander was only nineteen and looked even younger. Yet he spoke like a much older man. "It is a collegian!" people whispered to one another. From that day on, New Yorkers recognized Alexander as a voice in favor of revolution.

He also started writing articles arguing for independence in local newspapers. One of the things Alexander spoke about that day in the Fields was the Boston Tea Party.

Students at King's College knew that any day war might break out between the colonies and Great Britain. So they formed student groups and practiced military drills like soldiers. Alexander and his friends formed their own group called the Hearts of Oak. Alexander started studying military strategy in case he ever found himself on a real battlefield.

One night a mob formed in the streets of New York. They wanted to attack Dr. Myles Cooper because he supported the British. Although Alexander was in favor of independence, he was horrified at the idea of attacking someone just because they had different political views. Alexander vowed to protect him.

The Boston Tea Party

In Boston, on December 16, 1773, a group called the Sons of Liberty were protesting the Tea Act. The Tea Act gave the British the right to tax tea sold in America. On that December night, two hundred men dressed up like Mohawk Indians. They swarmed onto a British ship that had landed in Boston Harbor with a load of tea from Britain. The men dumped the tea over the side of the ship into the harbor.

The Boston Tea Party is one of the most famous acts of protest in American history.

He stood up to the crowd, telling them that violence would only hurt their cause. He couldn't stop the crowd, but he delayed them long enough for Dr. Myles Cooper to escape in his nightgown.

The Hearts of Oak

The students from King's College who practiced military drills in the cemetery of St. George's Chapel near the school before classes called themselves the Hearts of Oak. They wore uniforms they had designed themselves: short green jackets and hats with a knot of ribbons on the side.

They wore round leather caps with the slogan "Liberty or Death" and red tin hearts that read "God and Our Right." In 1775, the group rescued ten cannons from being captured by the British. The loyal Hearts of Oak remained friends for life.

In April 1775, the first real battle between British troops and the colonists took place in Massachusetts. In June of that year, George Washington was named commander of the American troops—the Continental Army. He marched through New York City on his way to Massachusetts. Alexander was in the crowd cheering him on.

In August of that year, a British warship arrived in New York Harbor. Everyone feared that the British would try to steal the two dozen cannons kept in New York. Alexander and fifteen members of the Hearts of Oak volunteered to attempt to hide the cannons. They saved ten big guns before the warship fired on them, frightening thousands of New Yorkers and sending them screaming into the streets.

After that success, it was not surprising when, six short months later, Alexander Hamilton was named a captain of artillery in New York's first official regiment. Alexander's dreams of one day being a war hero were on their way to becoming true.

CHAPTER 4
General Washington's Man

All of Alexander's studying about battle strategy and military exercises paid off when he became a captain in the army. People had already heard of his bravery in New York, and many military leaders wanted to work with him. The most important of these was none other than George Washington himself.

George Washington (1732–1799)

George Washington was born in Westmoreland County, Virginia. His father was a tobacco farmer who owned two plantations and many slaves. George inherited one of these properties, called Mount Vernon, after his father died. He became a major in the Virginia militia in his early twenties and fought in the French and Indian War. He sided with the Iroquois Indians against French colonists.

Washington was appointed commander in chief of the Continental Army in 1775. He was elected the first president of the United States in a landslide election in 1789 and served two terms before retiring. He died in 1799 of a fever. George Washington's portrait has been printed on the dollar bill since 1869.

Washington and Alexander fought together at the Battle of White Plains in October 1776. Two months later, on December 25, Alexander joined Washington in a surprise attack. In Trenton, New Jersey, there was a force of Hessians (say: HESH-ans)—German soldiers fighting for the British. Washington and his men were in Pennsylvania. Late at night they crossed the Delaware River that separated them from the British forces. The river was dangerous that time of year—icy and rough. It was a risk. But it paid off when Washington's troops defeated the Hessians and returned to Pennsylvania with all their supplies.

Alexander had been sick when Washington was planning the attack, but he got out of bed and led an eight-mile march through the snow to join his commander. Alexander always wanted to be out on the field fighting. He didn't like to sit on the sidelines. At this time, he commanded a regiment of sixty-eight men. Alexander was a popular leader. He expected hard work from the men in his regiment, but he was known for the respect he showed every one of them.

It was no surprise when a few weeks later Washington asked Alexander to be his assistant. General Washington also gave him a promotion to lieutenant colonel. Alexander was only twenty-two years old.

Another young man who made quite an impression on Washington was a nineteen-year-old Frenchman called the Marquis de Lafayette. Alexander and Lafayette quickly became good friends. Since Alexander could speak French, he could translate Lafayette's words for Washington.

On June 28, 1778, all three men—Alexander, Lafayette, and General Washington—fought together at the Battle of Monmouth in Freehold, New Jersey. It was a fierce battle. As Alexander rode into the fight, his horse was shot out right from under him, and he had to be carried off the field. But as the sun set, the British retreated and Alexander was reunited with his friends.

Marquis de Lafayette (1757–1834)

Marie-Joseph-Paul-Yves-Roch-Gilbert du Motier, known as the Marquis de Lafayette, was born in France to a wealthy family. He became a French military officer when he was only thirteen years old. Lafayette thought the American Revolution was a noble cause. Not only did he fight heroically in the American colonies as a major general in the Continental Army, he also raised money in France to help the cause.

When France had its own revolution in 1789, he became the commander in chief of the French

National Guard. Then the country turned against the National Guard. To avoid arrest, Lafayette fled to Austria, where he was captured and thrown into prison for five years. When Lafayette died in 1834, he was buried in Paris under soil from Bunker Hill, Massachusetts, the site of one of the most famous battles in the American Revolutionary War.

In the winter of 1780, Alexander was in Morristown, New Jersey, with the Continental Army. That is where he met Elizabeth "Eliza" Schuyler (say: SKY-ler). Eliza's father, Philip, was a general who lived in Albany, New York. He was very well known and wealthy. Philip Schuyler had three sons and four daughters at this time.

Elizabeth Schuyler

Eliza had come to Morristown to visit her aunt, but she soon became very interested in Alexander. He knew right away he wanted her to be his wife. In November, Alexander went to Albany to marry Eliza. He invited his father and brother to the wedding. But James and their father were still living in the West Indies, on two different islands.

Neither Alexander's father nor his brother could attend the wedding. But he was warmly

welcomed into the Schuyler family. Philip was proud of his new son-in-law, and Eliza's siblings loved him, too. For the first time since his mother's death, Alexander had a real family.

CHAPTER 5
The New Country

Being the assistant to George Washington was an important job. But Alexander was frustrated because General Washington was so protective of him. He wanted Alexander away from the battlefield, where he might get hurt. But Alexander dreamed of being a war hero. Finally he became so impatient that he actually quit his job as Washington's assistant! He and Eliza moved into a house on the east bank of the Hudson River, just opposite from Washington's headquarters.

Alexander continued to pester Washington to send him into battle.

Finally, Alexander got his wish. General Washington gave him command of a small unit of men. Alexander was ready to fight. Eliza returned to Albany. She was expecting their first

child. And Alexander couldn't stop thinking about the future.

What would happen when the country finally won its independence? He had many ideas. At that time, the thirteen American colonies worked independently of one another. The war was the first thing that had really united them all. The American government in 1781—the Continental Congress—was organized under what was called the Articles of Confederation.

Alexander thought that if America was going to be an independent nation, it would need a strong central government. That way the states could all work together. He thought the government should have a bank of its own that could lend and borrow money for the new country. He studied the banking systems of other countries, like Great Britain, to plan a system of money and banking for America.

The Articles of Confederation

The Articles of Confederation was an agreement among all thirteen colonies to act as one nation 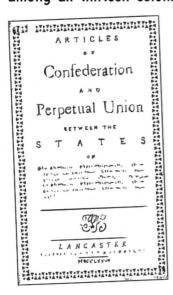 in order to fight the Revolutionary War. It also helped to streamline the way the colonies dealt with the foreign governments of other countries. It was the first model of government for the United States. But there were many things the Articles did not cover, such as the establishment of taxes and laws. In many ways, the Articles of Confederation did not create a central government, because the individual colonies still kept all their power.

In October 1781, Alexander was sent to Yorktown, Virginia. There he and Lafayette met up with General Washington. The British commander, General Cornwallis, had stationed his troops nearby. On the night of October 14, Alexander led his men on a charge against the British troops. The Continental Army won. Cornwallis's surrender to General Washington signaled that the British had given up.

Although the war went on for two more years, the battle at Yorktown is usually seen as the turning point—the beginning of the end—for British rule in America. Alexander was a hero. He was also a father! Eliza had a son named Philip on January 22, 1782. Alexander couldn't wait to get home to be with them. The family all lived in the Schuyler mansion in Albany with Eliza's parents.

The Schuyler mansion

Alexander then devoted himself to studying law and soon earned a license to be a lawyer in New York. Often he worked with Aaron Burr, who had also become a lawyer. Alexander surprised many people by sometimes working for Tories. These were people who had supported the British during the Revolutionary War. They hadn't wanted the American colonies to become independent. Many people felt the Tories had no right to expect an American lawyer to defend them. But Alexander thought everyone deserved equal rights in the courts, no matter what they believed. He also often defended poor people who couldn't afford to pay him.

He knew what it was like to be poor and not be able to defend himself. He wanted better for other people.

Just as Alexander had predicted, it was hard for the country to continue operating under the Articles of Confederation. For instance, the northern states had spent a lot of money during the war. The southern states had not spent as much because most of the fighting had been in the North. If there was a strong central government, Alexander thought, it could distribute the debt—the money that had been borrowed and was now owed—equally. Since the war was fought for everyone, this was only fair. But under the Articles of Confederation, the states could still decide for themselves, and the southern states did not want to pay for the North.

In 1782, Alexander met a new friend who agreed with his ideas for a central government. His name was James Madison. Madison was representing his home state of Virginia. Hamilton was representing New York. Each man supported the other's ideas about the country needing a strong central government.

Alexander, Eliza, and Philip moved to New York City in 1783. Alexander was very interested in the finances of his home state of New York. America was a young country with hardly any banks. The Bank of North America was established in Philadelphia in 1781. Alexander wanted to set up the same type of bank in New York, one that would lend notes (paper money) as well as gold and silver. Alexander's Bank of New York opened in 1784 and is still operating today.

The Bank of New York, 1784

By 1787, Alexander's family had grown. He had three children, Philip, Angelica, and Alexander, and an adopted daughter, Fanny. The country had come to agree with him that they needed a different government to replace the Articles of Confederation. But would this new government be any better than the last? Alexander was determined to make sure that it would.

CHAPTER 6
The Federalist Papers

Alexander and his friend James Madison wanted to explain exactly why America needed a strong bank and a central government. They wanted a ruling body for the country that could tax each state in order to raise money. They laid out their ideas for how the new government would work in a series of essays they called the Federalist Papers. The word *federal* meant an agreement between people. The word *federalist* meant the colonies should unite and form a more powerful government together in addition to each state's own governing group. Alexander wanted the states to agree to one central government.

The Federalist Papers called for a government with three branches: a president (executive), a congress (legislative), and a supreme court (judicial). As members of the Continental Congress, Alexander and James Madison were not allowed to talk about this subject publicly.

So no one at the time knew who was writing the Federalist Papers, but everyone was reading them in the newspapers. When the Constitution for the new government was finally written, many of its ideas came from Alexander's and James's eighty-five Federalist Papers. They describe much of what our federal government is today.

The Constitution itself was written by many people working together, including James

Madison, John Adams, Thomas Jefferson, and Alexander Hamilton. In order for the Constitution to become the basis of a new government, it had to be agreed to by at least nine out of the thirteen states. People who supported the new Constitution became known as Federalists because they wanted a strong federal (united and central) government. Those who didn't want it were called Anti-

Federalists. One by one, the states agreed to the new Constitution.

When New York voted yes, they held a big celebration. Even though they didn't know Alexander had written many of the Federalist Papers, his defense of the Constitution was so well-known that they honored him along with it.

The new government became official in July 1788, just a few months after Alexander and Eliza had their fourth child, James. This new government would need a president, and Alexander knew exactly who it should be: George Washington.

In 1789, George Washington won by a landslide. John Adams became the vice president.

Washington had to choose men to help him run the government. These advisors were known as his cabinet. One of the cabinet positions was for a secretary of the treasury, who would be in charge of financial matters. Washington's first choice was Robert Morris, the former superintendent of finance. Morris turned down the job, but he suggested Alexander for the position.

Robert Morris

The First US Election

The very first presidential election was held from December 15, 1788, to January 10, 1789. Of the three million people living in the United States at that time, less than 1.3 percent voted.

Votes were cast only by electors. These were men appointed or elected by each state. A state got the same number of electors as they were assigned seats in Congress. (Two states, North Carolina and Rhode Island, couldn't participate because they hadn't yet agreed to the Constitution. New York also did not vote, because it had not been able to decide on its electors.)

The person who got the most votes from the state-chosen electors became president. The person who came in second, with the next largest number of votes, was elected the vice president.

Washington was surprised. Even though he
loved Alexander like
a son, he had no
idea Alexander knew
anything about
finances, banking,
or economics! When
he offered him the
job, Alexander happily
accepted. He quit his

law practice so that he could focus entirely on his
role within the new government.

Alexander also thought that if he was going
to work for the government, he should not have
any other job, because that might prevent him
from being fair to everyone. For instance, people
he had defended as a lawyer might expect him
to support laws that helped them more than
others. And he didn't want any of his clients or
old associates asking for favors.

George Washington was sworn in as president on April 30, 1789. The new government of the United States of America was now official. At thirty-four years old, Alexander Hamilton was its first secretary of the treasury. He was eager to serve his country.

CHAPTER 7
Secretary of the Treasury

In 1789, the United States government was set up just the way it is today. The First Congress had already been in session since March. It was made up of a Senate and a House of Representatives that made laws. The Senate had two representatives for each of the thirteen states. The House of Representatives had different numbers of congressmen from each state, based on how many people lived there. The first Supreme Court met on February 2, 1790. It was the court's job to

decide whether a law followed the rules that had been established by the Constitution.

Alexander was the secretary of the treasury. The treasury is a place where money is kept, but it can also mean the money itself. He advised President Washington on all kinds of money matters and financial decisions. Thomas Jefferson was the secretary of state. He advised the president on US relations with foreign countries.

People both in the United States and around the world quickly came to see that Alexander Hamilton was one of the most important people in the new country. Many remembered him as a war hero at Yorktown. But he was now famous as Washington's most trusted advisor and one of the creators of the government.

Alexander had a lot of ideas about the US Treasury. For example, he thought the federal government should pay off all the money that the individual states had borrowed as loans during the Revolutionary War. In order to do this, there would need to be a federal bank—a government-run bank that would collect taxes.

Paper money issued by the Continental Congress

Some states, especially in the South, had already paid off their debts by 1789. They didn't think it was fair that other people shouldn't have to do the same. Other states, especially in the North, thought Alexander's idea was good because most of the fighting had been done there. Therefore, their governments had spent more money to fund the army. Why shouldn't the whole country help pay it off, when it was everyone's war?

Alexander hoped to use taxes to pay off these debts. He especially wanted to tax imports arriving from other countries. This, too, worried some people in the South. Although their economy was based on selling and exporting cotton to other countries, they were afraid that these new taxes would cause other countries to tax American cotton in return. They thought Alexander was giving the North an unfair advantage.

Alexander thought that if America had a bank that was strong enough to loan and borrow money, it would show that the United States could do the same for other countries as well. He felt that having a federal bank was the only way to compete with other countries, like England.

In February 1790, Alexander made a speech to
Congress explaining his financial plans. A few days
later, he was surprised and hurt when his friend
James Madison made a speech that criticized it.
Alexander felt very betrayed.

People in the government—and all around the country—were starting to fall into two groups when it came to how they thought America should be run. The Federalists believed in Alexander's ideas. They also thought the United States should have a strong relationship with England because England's government was much like the one they had built.

FEDERALIST VS ANTI-FEDERALIST

The Anti-Federalists became known as the Democratic-Republicans. These included Thomas Jefferson and James Madison, who had by then changed his mind about Alexander's ideas. They believed in strong state governments and an economy based on farming, and they wanted a close relationship with France. The Democratic-Republicans did not like how close Alexander was to George Washington. The president seemed to listen to his advice on everything. For a few months in 1790, Washington got very sick, and Alexander even seemed to take over for him—just as he had taken over the trading floor as a boy in the Caribbean.

The newspapers were filled with articles and letters written by people on both the Federalist and the Anti-Federalist sides. Sometimes they personally attacked the men in the government. And one article accused Alexander of using his role in the government to make money for himself. This was especially hard for Alexander to hear because he thought it was so important for him to be honest with America's money. He had even quit his law practice to be fair—which made it harder for him to support his growing family.

In 1792, Eliza and Alexander had a fifth child, John Church Hamilton.

That same year, Washington was elected for a second term as president. By this time, Alexander had moved his family from Wall Street to Market Street in Philadelphia. Their new home was near the presidential mansion where George Washington lived.

From 1789 to 1790, New York City was the capital of the United States. Although Washington, DC, had been declared the capital in 1790, the city was not yet built. The new capital city would not be ready until 1800. Until

The President's House on Market Street

that time, the federal government would be based in Philadelphia

In 1793, there was an outbreak of yellow fever in Philadelphia. Over four thousand people died. Alexander and Eliza both got sick. They went to stay at a summer house they owned outside the city. The children were sent to the Schuyler home, further north in Albany, so they wouldn't get sick.

Alexander's childhood friend, Edward Stevens, was now a doctor. He rushed to their home to treat the Hamiltons. Because he had grown up in St. Croix, where yellow fever was common,

Yellow Fever

Yellow fever is a fast-spreading and far-reaching contagious disease. It is carried by mosquitoes and originally spread from Africa throughout the route of the slave trade. Yellow fever makes a person's muscles ache and their skin and the  whites of their eyes turn a sickly yellow color. The color is brought on by damage to the patient's liver. Stagnant water, and especially bad sewage systems that attract mosquitoes, spread the disease quickly.

The largest yellow fever outbreaks in the United States occurred in 1793 and during the 1850s.

Edward had different ideas about how to treat the disease. While some doctors were draining their patients' blood, Edward's methods encouraged them to rest and get stronger.

Alexander and Eliza both recovered. Alexander was so grateful to his friend Edward, he wrote a letter to the newspaper about how everyone should use Dr. Stevens's treatments.

But even this was turned into a political fight. Democratic-Republicans claimed Alexander hadn't even been sick! They said he was faking all along, and that the letter was written to promote Dr. Stevens's business.

All this political fighting was very tiring. It was not surprising when both Alexander and Thomas Jefferson decided to leave their government jobs. Alexander left his position as secretary of the treasury in January 1795. Although he was only forty, he planned to retire from the government to be with his family and work as a lawyer. But Alexander could never stay on the sidelines for long.

CHAPTER 8
At Home

The Grange

Now that he had left his government job, Alexander decided to move his family to a new house called the Grange. The house was in Harlem, farther north in Manhattan. In 1795, the neighborhood of Harlem was practically considered the country! Alexander named the house the Grange after his father's family's castle in Scotland. Alexander had not seen his father since he was eleven years old, but Alexander had sent money to him.

After leaving office, Alexander took a three-week trip around Cayuga Lake in New York State to meet the Native people there. Alexander had often tried to use his influence in the government to protect the rights of American Indians.

He helped manage a school that taught both English and American Indian languages. When he returned to the city, he immediately began his law practice once again.

That same year, Alexander received an unexpected letter. It was from the Hamiltons of Scotland, his father's family. They, like the rest of the world, had been watching the formation of this new country and knew that their famous relative had played a role in it. After years of ignoring Alexander because his father was not married to his mother, Alexander's noble Scottish relatives wanted to meet him! Of course he was happy to invite them to visit him in New York.

In the spring of 1796, after seven years of being president, George Washington decided to retire. He asked Alexander to write his Farewell Address. The speech was published on September 19, 1796, and was immediately reprinted in all the newspapers. It is the most famous letter to the nation Washington ever published, but for years, no one knew it was written by Alexander Hamilton!

Washington's Farewell Address

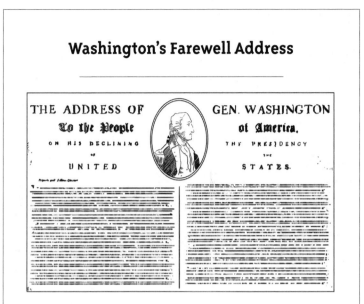

George Washington was America's first president and a very popular one. Many people couldn't imagine how the country would be run with anyone else doing the job! So Washington's Farewell Address was very important. In it, he said that if he had been a good president, it was because he had had the support of the American people. Americans were the real strength of their country, and they needed to stick together in order to make it work. The nation did not need *him* to succeed. They needed one another.

John Adams was sworn in as the second president of the United States on March 4, 1797. But Alexander was no longer a part of the president's cabinet. He was happy just to be spending time with his family. Eliza's sister Angelica, who had been living in England with her husband for years, returned to America, and Alexander and Eliza were very happy to see her again. In August 1797, Alexander and Eliza had another son, William Steven.

The Hamiltons had six children, the oldest now fifteen. They were close to both Eliza's family and to Alexander's relatives. They enjoyed welcoming family—and anyone else who needed a place to stay—into their home. For a man who once had no one, Alexander was now surrounded by people who loved him.

CHAPTER 9
Unexpected Tragedy

In September 1798, New York City was hit with a yellow fever epidemic. Alexander's family was spared this time, but people all over New York were still frightened. Nearly forty-five people were dying each day in the city.

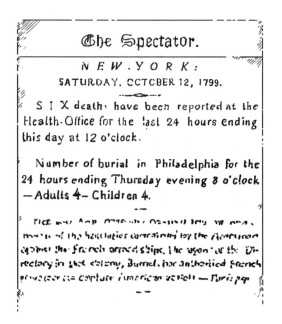

People did not yet understand that yellow fever was spread by mosquitoes. But they did know that standing water and unsanitary conditions

Aaron Burr

made the epidemic worse. Many people drank dirty or polluted water because they had no access to clean water. In 1799, Aaron Burr proposed to do something about this. At that time, Aaron Burr was employed by the government of New York State. He wanted to start the Manhattan Company. This new business would lay pipes to bring clean water to the people living in the lower end—the southern tip—of New York City. Alexander thought this was a great idea and supported Aaron's plan.

But the truth was that Aaron Burr had other plans besides bringing clean water to everyone. The real purpose of the Manhattan Company was to raise money by telling people it was for clean water, but then only use a part of that money for the job. The rest would be available to the organizers of the plan, men like Aaron Burr. A single clause of the company's charter—the document that set the rules for what the company could do—allowed the Manhattan Company to use any money it wasn't using for water for other kinds of banking business.

In New York at that time, there were only two banks. One was the state bank that belonged to the government. The other was the Bank of New York, which Alexander Hamilton had helped to start. Aaron Burr wanted to become an important man in New York. He chose to create his own bank that would lend him money whenever he asked for it. It could also make him a lot of money. The

Manhattan Company raised $2 million for its water system, but only used $100,000 to actually provide water! People continued to get sick.

Alexander was furious. From that moment on, he knew that Aaron Burr was a dishonest man. So he was not happy when Thomas Jefferson was elected president in 1801 with none other than Aaron Burr as his vice president!

Alexander and Eliza now had seven children. Their daughter, Elizabeth Holly, also known as Eliza, had been born in 1799. By 1801, their oldest son, Philip, was a handsome, charming young man of nineteen who was very loyal to his father. When

Philip Hamilton

a man named George Eacker gave a speech that insulted Alexander, Philip confronted him about it. Eacker called Philip a "rascal." This was a very serious word in 1801. Philip demanded an apology. Eacker refused. Philip wasted no time and quickly challenged Eacker to a duel.

When Philip talked to his father about the duel, Alexander suggested that he should "throw

Dueling

In the late eighteenth and early nineteenth centuries, dueling was a popular way for gentlemen to settle their differences. If two men disagreed with each other, they would have friends—known as "seconds"—try to work out a truce between them by passing messages back and forth. Usually this worked. But if it did not, the two men would stand a certain distance apart and each fire a single

gunshot at each other. If they were lucky, both walked away uninjured. But often they were not.

Dueling was dangerous and often illegal, but wealthy men still met in secret and held duels. Any man who refused to duel would be labeled a coward.

away" his first shot. He meant that Philip should not shoot directly *at* Eacker. When Eacker realized this, he would then also fire his pistol in the air instead of at Philip. What kind of man, Alexander thought, would shoot someone who wasn't shooting at them?

Philip followed his father's advice. Unfortunately, Eacker did not. Philip was shot and carried to the house of one of his aunts. Alexander and Eliza rushed to his side. Eliza was pregnant with their eighth child. Philip died the day after the duel.

Six months later, in June 1802, Eliza gave birth to their final child, a son. They named him

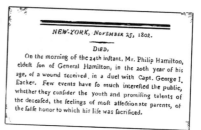

Philip after the older brother he would never know. Alexander loved his new son, whom he called "Little Phil," but he knew their family would never be the same. From then on, Alexander was a sadder, more troubled man.

CHAPTER 10
Legacy

The entire Hamilton family was heartbroken after Philip's death. For months Alexander couldn't think about anything else. But slowly he went back to work as a lawyer.

Aaron Burr was still vice president. He did not think he would be reelected, so instead he ran for governor of New York in 1804. Of course, Alexander still considered Burr to be a dishonest man. He supported Burr's opponent in the election, Morgan Lewis. When Aaron Burr lost the race for governor, he put some of the blame on Alexander.

In March 1804, Alexander went to dinner at the house of a friend, John Tayler. Over dinner, the men talked about many things, including

Aaron Burr. Afterward, another of the dinner guests—Dr. Charles Cooper—wrote a letter to his brother telling him all about his dinner with the great Alexander Hamilton. In the letter, he mentioned that Alexander had called Aaron Burr untrustworthy. Somehow this letter got into the hands of a newspaper publisher who immediately printed it in his paper for the whole city to read.

Many people said they didn't believe Alexander would say such a thing. But Dr. Cooper said it was all true. In fact, he said that he knew an even more "despicable" thing that Alexander had said. He was hinting that Alexander had said even worse things about Aaron Burr that night!

Aaron Burr demanded an apology. Alexander refused. Their two friends, Nathaniel Pendleton and William P. Van Ness, tried to work out a peace between the two men, but they couldn't. Alexander and Burr decided to fight a duel.

Alexander did not tell his family about the duel. He quietly finished up all the law cases he was working on so that his business would be settled and his clients would not need him for anything. He told a few close friends that he planned to not shoot at Aaron Burr. Since his son Philip's death, he just couldn't bring himself to shoot at another man. He wrote goodbye letters to his family in case he didn't survive the duel.

On July 11, 1804, Alexander and his second, Nathaniel Pendleton, rowed across the river to Weehawken, New Jersey. This was the same spot where Philip had been killed three years earlier. The duel was set for seven o'clock in the morning. The only other person there beside the two men and their seconds was Dr. David Hosack. Alexander chose to stand on the north side of the clearing, facing the sun. Each man had a flintlock pistol—the same type Philip used in his duel—that had been borrowed from Alexander's brother-in-law John Church.

The two men raised their guns and fired. Alexander's shot, as he planned, landed nowhere near Aaron Burr. It hit a tree. Burr shot Alexander above the hip. He fell to the ground. Nathaniel Pendleton and Dr. Hosack carried Alexander to the boat and rushed him back across the river to the city. William P. Van Ness hurried Aaron Burr away from the scene so that he wouldn't be arrested.

Alexander was taken to the house of a friend, William Bayard. Soon his whole family was gathered around him. By the next afternoon, he had died from his injury. All the businesses in New York City closed for his funeral. New Yorkers wore black armbands in his memory. The New York Supreme Court draped its bench in black fabric for the rest of its term.

Alexander Hamilton's funeral was the grandest the city had ever seen. Many in the crowd were angry. They thought Aaron Burr should have been punished.

Eliza did not attend her husband's funeral. She was too sad to leave the house. Alexander had left her a letter saying that he loved her and their family, ending with, "Adieu best of wives and

Walpol

SATURDAY, JULY 21, 1804.

DUEL.

DIED, at New-York, on the afternoon of the 12th inst. General ALEXANDER HAMILTON, of a wound which he received on the morning of the preceding day in a duel with Col. BURR. Never was a death more sincerely and justly lamented: and his loss will be sensibly felt throughout the United States

When the feelings of the public shall, in some measure have subsided, we shall probably present to our readers a correct statement of the circumstances which produced this melancholy event, together with a tribute of respect to the unequalled talents and virtues of that great and illustrious character.

[Cent.]

best of women. Embrace all my darling children for me." Eliza would devote the rest of her life to protecting her husband's memory.

Aaron Burr never went to jail and never said he was sorry. He often referred to Alexander as "my friend Hamilton—whom I shot." People were shocked at how little he seemed to care about what he had done. Some were so angry, they threatened to burn down Burr's house. His reputation never recovered. One newspaper editor in Charleston, South Carolina, said that Burr's heart was stuffed with "cinders raked from the fires of hell."

Burr became worried that he would be arrested for murder, so he fled New York and moved to Philadelphia.

The enormous influence of Alexander Hamilton is still felt today. We continue to rely on the national banking system that he established. And the Bank of New York, which he founded, is

 the oldest bank in the United States. Because of his role as the first secretary of the treasury, his portrait is on the ten-dollar bill. The Federalist Papers, Alexander's brilliant framework for how the US government should be run, is still quoted by our Supreme Court justices.

In 2015, a new musical called *Hamilton* debuted in New York City. The show was based on a biography of Alexander Hamilton that was written by Ron Chernow.

Alexander Hamilton was not born in the United States. But he made the country his home. In some ways, he shaped our system of

government and our country more than any of the other founding fathers. He arrived in the American colonies with nothing, and became one of the most important men in American history. We will always be in his debt.

Hamilton the Musical

Hamilton: An American Musical was written by Lin-Manuel Miranda, who also starred in the show as Alexander Hamilton. Born in New York City to a Puerto Rican family, Lin-Manuel thought Alexander Hamilton had a lot in common with modern immigrants to America. The show he wrote about Alexander Hamilton's life features

all kinds of music, including hip-hop and rap. He cast the musical almost entirely with non-white actors. By doing this, he claimed the founding fathers and American history for *all* Americans.

Hamilton won a Grammy award for Best Musical

Theater Album and the Pulitzer Prize for Drama in 2016. The show won eleven Tony Awards, but it had been nominated for sixteen—more than any other Broadway show in history.

Timeline of Alexander Hamilton's Life

1755	Alexander Hamilton is born in Nevis, British West Indies
1768	Mother dies
1773	Sails to America
1774	Enters King's College, New York City
1776	Joins the Continental Army
1777	Joins George Washington's staff
1780	Marries Elizabeth Schuyler
1781	Fights in the Battle of Yorktown as a lieutenant colonel
1782	First son, Philip, is born in New York
1783	Opens a law practice in New York
1784	Founds the Bank of New York
1789	Becomes the first secretary of the treasury
1796	Writes George Washington's Farewell Address
1801	Son Philip dies in a duel
	Last child, also named Philip, is born
1804	Dies in New York City after a duel with Aaron Burr

Timeline of the World

1754	The gas carbon dioxide is discovered by Scottish scientist Joseph Black
1761	The tune of "Twinkle, Twinkle Little Star" is published in France
1766	Series of deadly wolf attacks in France causes people to believe a monster is stalking the country
1773	French astronomer discovers the spiral Whirlpool Galaxy, twenty-three million light years from Earth
1776	Declaration of Independence is signed in Philadelphia
1782	The bald eagle is chosen as the emblem of the United States
1789	French Revolution begins
1790	First lifeboat tested in England
1791	Composer Wolfgang Amadeus Mozart dies in Austria
1796	First smallpox vaccination given in England
1801	The dwarf planet Ceres is discovered by an Italian monk
1802	Marie Tussaud exhibits her first wax sculptures in England, including King Louis XVI and Marie Antoinette of France
1804	Haiti becomes independent from France in the only successful slave revolt in history

Bibliography

* Books for young readers

* Brown, Don. *Aaron and Alexander: The Most Famous Duel in American History*. New York: Roaring Brook Press, 2015.

Chernow, Ron. *Alexander Hamilton*. New York: Penguin Books, 2004.

* Fradin, Dennis Brindell. *Duel! Burr and Hamilton's Deadly War of Words*. New York: Walker and Co., 2008.

* Fritz, Jean. *Alexander Hamilton, The Outsider*. New York: Penguin Books, 2011.

"Hamilton's Financial Plan" *U.S. History: Pre-Columbian to the New Millennium*. http://www.ushistory.org/us/18b.asp.

Krugman, Paul. "In Hamilton's Debt." *New York Times*, April 22, 2016.

Miranda, Lin-Manuel. *Hamilton: An American Musical: Original Broadway Cast Recording*. Atlantic, 2015, compact disc.

Pollack, Michael. "Answers to Questions about New York." *New York Times*, July 8, 2011.

Randall, Willard Sterne. *Alexander Hamilton: A Life*. New York: HarperCollins, 2003.

* St. George, Judith. *The Duel: The Parallel Lives of Alexander Hamilton and Aaron Burr*. New York: Penguin Group, 2009.